M

SAINT MAGNUS

EDITED AND PRESENTED BY IAIN MACDONALD

FLORIS BOOKS

First published in 1993 by Floris Books

© Floris Books, Edinburgh 1993

The publisher acknowledges subsidy from the
Scottish Arts Council towards the publication
of this volume.

British Library CIP Data available

ISBN 0-86315-164-7

Printed in Great Britain
by BPCC Wheatons Ltd, Exeter

Contents

Introduction

The sacking of Lindisfarne in 793 announced in the British Isles a wave of Norse aggression, piracy and conquest which was to endure for some three hundred years. It was not just the savagery, but also the speed and surprise of the Viking raids from the sea, which caused fear and dread. Norse shipbuilding skills had produced what was probably the most effective instrument of sea-going warfare since the Roman galley: the fast, shallow-draught longship, able to penetrate far up tidal rivers, and as manoeuvrable by oar against the wind as it was by sail before it. These robust but flexible wooden craft carried the Viking adventurers across the Atlantic to Iceland, Greenland and North America; through the Bay of Biscay and down the coasts of Spain to the Mediterranean, reaching Sicily and possibly Constantinople; and across the Baltic into the fjords, rivers and lakes of Finland and Russia.

Soon, the coasts of Britain, Ireland, and even France, were to experience the scourge of the sea-borne raiders. The monk Alcuin wrote: "Never before in Britain has such a terror appeared as this we have now suffered at the hands of the heathen." In the sixty years after the *sacking of Lindisfarne, the monasteries of Jarrow and Iona, the cities of York, London and even Winchester, would all suffer in their turn.*

By the ninth century, the Vikings had established permanent settlements around the British Isles and Faroes, and as far west as Iceland, where many Norsemen fled to escape quarrels at home. In Orkney, Shetland and the western isles, regular trade routes and political ties were maintained with Norway and its rulers, in whose gift the earldoms of the isles were kept. The farmlands, fishing waters and harbours of the Orkney islands, in particular, represented both a rich levying ground and a springboard for launching raids further south and west.

During the eleventh century, Norway was converted to Christianity under King Olaf Haraldsson and King Knut (Canute) the Great, whose military and political skills brought him to the throne of England as well as those of Norway and Denmark, establishing, almost, an Anglo-Scandinavian empire. During this period, closer cultural bonds with Europe and a more effective rule of civil and ecclesiastical law were created throughout the world of Norse influence.

However with Knut's death the great age of Viking hegemony overseas was already on the wane. Following the defeat of Harald Hardradi at the battle of Stamford

Bridge in 1066, Norse power shrank back to little more than a succession of harassing expeditions, which however persisted right up to the thirteenth century. Magnus Barelegs made three westward "hostings," on one of which the young Magnus Erlendsson made himself noteworthy by singing psalms during the battle of the Menai Strait.

The Norse earldom endured in Orkney until the mid-fifteenth century when it was pledged to the Scottish crown for 50,000 florins by the debt-stricken Christian I, a pledge which has never been redeemed. The "Viking Isles" retain a Scandinavian character and orientation which are quite distinctive in Scotland to the present day.

Magnus Erlendsson was born in 1075 of a noble line of earls in Orkney, related to the Norwegian kings. His grandfather was Earl Thorfinn, greatest of the Orkney earls, and his father, Erlend, fought in the ill-fated battle of Stamford Bridge in 1066, in which the final Norse attempt on the English throne came to nothing.

Magnus himself, as the present account makes clear, was hardly saintly in his young manhood when he participated in raids and murders beside his brother Vikings. Even as a ruler, he was not above ruthlessness, as incidents during his commonwealth with Earl Hakon reveal. However, the author takes pains to assure us that "Magnus had these things done, not as a viking or robber, but as a just ruler of a province and a guardian of the laws."

It seems to have been, in the end, Magnus' very refusal to pursue aggression for its own sake, perhaps the distinctive quality of the Viking lifestyle, which produced his own death and subsequent reputation as a saint. In his resistance to war and bloodlust, Magnus' martyrdom represents a choice of path which was all too vital and relevant for his time. The new way of Christianity, with its civilizing implications, still had an uncertain hold, and even in Magnus' time, efforts were being made "to root out the evils which had long attended heathenism." These affected the very fabric of society, its customs and arrangements, quite apart from the old ways of piracy and plunder which continued to beckon strongly, upheld in the songs and traditions guarding the reputations of the pagan gods and heroes. Magnus' death was therefore the assertion of a new kind of power, a power that was to heal and bind in order to rule. Hakon himself, the murderer, turned his life towards the new path. He became a pilgrim to the Holy Land, and returning to Orkney, established himself as a much-loved and just ruler.

The Orkneyinga Saga tells how Magnus' nephew,

Earl Rognvald, vowed that, being restored to his rightful realm of Orkney, he would have a church of stone built in Kirkwall as a shrine to the relics of his uncle, "so that there be none more magnificent in the land." The building of the new cathedral began in 1137, supervised by Kol, Rognvald's father. It is thought that the masons employed in the work came from Durham.

In 1919, human remains were uncovered in the stonework of the pier on the south side of the cathedral choir, the skull bearing marks corresponding to the death-wound received by Magnus at Egilsay. The relics were restored to the same resting-place where they are today. Earl St Rognvald's relics, discovered in the nineteenth century, rest in the pier on the north side of the choir.

St Magnus' feast-day is celebrated on April 16, which is traditionally kept as the day of his martyrdom in 1116.

There are three versions of Magnus's life, all of which owe something to the work of Master Robert, who apparently wrote some twenty years after Magnus' death, around the time of the initial construction of the new cathedral in Kirkwall. Robert's Latin Vita is lost but it was rendered into Icelandic. One version has come down in the Orkneyinga Saga, where we find the most complete description of Magnus as a person. There are two other versions, both written in Iceland, known as the Lesser Saga and the Greater Saga. The second of these forms the main basis of the present text, though the account of Bishop William's reluctance to accept the sainthood of Magnus is taken from the Lesser Saga, as well as the story of Gunni's dream and the cure of Eldjarn in the new St Magnus church.

The present translation, shortened and edited for this edition, was included in W.M. Metcalfe's Ancient Lives of the Scottish Saints, published by Alexander Gardner at Paisley in 1895.

The life of St Magnus

Of the birth of the holy Magnus, Earl Erlend's son; and how, quarrels arising between the earls of Orkney, then Hakon, Magnus's cousin, departed to Norway and Sweden.

In the days of Harold Sigurdsson, King of Norway, there ruled over Orkney as Earls, two brothers, Paul and Erlend, the sons of Thorfinn, the most powerful of all the Earls of Orkney. He was son of Earl Sigurd whom King Olaf Tryggvisson converted, along with all the people of Orkney, to the Christian faith. This Sigurd fell at the battle of Clontarf in Ireland.

Earl Erlend married a woman called Thora, daughter to Summarlid Ospaksson. The sons of Earl Erlend and Thora were Magnus and Erling, and his daughters were Gunnhild and Cecilia.

Earl Paul, Erlend's brother, married a daughter of Earl Hakon, son of Ivar and Ragnhild, daughter of King Magnus the Good, son of King Olaf the Holy. Paul's son was called Hakon, who afterwards comes into the story.

The holy Magnus was born in Orkney, the

most noble of race and illustrious of kindred. And
though with many, greatness of birth is turned to
pride and spoiling of temper, yet this blessed child
loved, honoured and preserved the highest virtue,
a kindly nature, gentle manners, and steadfastness
in honourable ways.

At an early age the boy was sent to school to
learn the sacred Scriptures and the other knowledge that men then most studied. Magnus was
gentle and tractable, docile and obedient to his
father and mother and teachers; kind and dear to
all the people. He attached himself little to wickedness and pastimes as other young men, but
conducted himself in a seemly way, though he was
young in years; for there shone in him the manifest gift of the Holy Spirit, which guided him to
all good things.

While the brothers, Erlend and Paul, held rule
in Orkney, there came west from Norway King
Harald Sigurdsson with a mighty army. The Earls
resolved to accompany the King south to England: and in the battle that they fought with King
Harald Godwinsson, there fell Harald Sigurdsson,
the fifth night after St Matthew's day, in the
autumn. After this battle Olaf the Quiet, Harald's
son, sailed with the Earls that autumn back to

Orkney. Olaf passed the winter in Orkney, and was the best of friends with the Earls, his kinsmen, for his brother's daughters were Thora, Olaf's mother, and Ingibiorg, the mother of the Earls. Olaf went in the spring east to Norway, and was there made King with Magnus, his brother.

These brothers, Paul and Erlend, ruled Orkney a long time, and long was their agreement good. But when their sons began to grow up, Hakon and Erling became very overbearing, but Magnus was the quietest and best mannered in everything. All the kinsmen were men of large stature, strong, and highly accomplished in all things. Hakon, Paul's son, wished to be overman to Erlend's sons, because he thought he was of better birth than they; for he was daughter's son to Earl Hakon Ivarsson and Ragnhild, daughter of King Magnus the Good, as was told before.

So it came about that they began not to agree; for many men inclined to Erlend's sons, and would not have them held inferior to any in the islands, for they were of all the people better liked and beloved. This was a cause of great offence to Hakon all his life. The sons of the Earls were never safe with each other. Their fathers tried to arrange matters for them, so that they might be at peace.

A meeting was called, and it was soon found that each Earl favoured his own sons, and they began not to agree. Then great quarrels arose between these brothers, and so they parted. Next went men between them to make peace, and a meeting was called between them in Hrossey. At this meeting they were reconciled on this condition, that the islands should be divided into two equal parts; and so things stood for a while. Hakon, Paul's son, greatly molested the men who served Erlend and his sons, so much so that it seemed to them that they could not endure it; and so they began to quarrel, and marched against each other with many men.

Havard Gunnisson and other chiefs and friends of the Earls then tried to make peace between them, but Erlend and his sons would come to no agreement if Hakon was to remain in the islands. But as it seemed to their friends that there would be great danger if they were not reconciled to each other, Hakon left the islands at once; and then an agreement was come to between those brothers on the advice of good men.

Hakon first went east to Norway to see King Olaf the Quiet; it was towards the end of his days; he dwelt there a short time. Thence he went east to Sweden to see King Ingi Steinkelsson, and was well received by him for some time.

How Hakon sought out a soothsayer; and persuaded King Magnus Barelegs of Norway to take a host to Orkney.

Christianity was then young in Sweden: there were many who practised the old magic, by which they thought to become acquainted with things not yet come to pass. King Ingi was a good Christian, and took great pains to root out the evils which had long attended heathenism.

When Hakon Paulsson was in Sweden, he heard tell that there was in the land a man who dealt in divination and soothsaying, whether by witchcraft or other means. Hakon was anxious to meet this man, and to see what he could learn about his fate. He went in search of him and found him in a certain forest country, where he used to go about from feast to feast, and tell the franklins of the seasons and other matters about which they were curious. When Hakon found this man he inquired of him how it would go with him for power or other fortune. The soothsayer asked him who he was. He told him his name and family, that he was daughter's son to Earl Hakon, son of Ivar.

Then answered the soothsayer: "Why would you have knowledge or soothsaying of me? Do you not know that your former kinsmen have had little faith in the kind of men that I am?"

Hakon replied: "I have come to you because I feel that neither of us has any need to look down upon the other because of virtue or religion."

The man answered: "You shall have this service from me. Come to me on the third night and we two shall then see whether I am able to tell you some of the things you are anxious to learn."

After this they parted, and Hakon remained there in the district. And after three nights he came again to the soothsayer. He was then in a certain house alone, and breathed heavily when Hakon went in, and wiped his forehead, and said that he had had to struggle hard before he became wise in the things he wanted to foresee.

He said then: "If you would know your fate and about your life, it is long to tell: for from your faring west to Orkney very great events will come to pass when all the things to which they lead are fulfilled. And I have a presentiment that one day you will eventually become sole ruler of Orkney, though to you it may seem long to wait. I also think that your descendants will remain there. You will also in your lifetime cause a crime to be done for which you may or may not be forgiven by the God in whom you trust. But your steps lie further out into the world than I can see, yet I think that you will bring back your bones to these northern parts."

Hakon answered: "Great things you tell me, if they are true; but I think it will go better with me, as possibly you have not seen these things in their truth."

The soothsayer bade him believe what he liked of it. And on this they parted.

And when Hakon had been a little while with King Ingi, he sailed to Norway to see King Magnus Barelegs, his kinsman; there he heard tidings from Orkney that Earl Erlend and his sons mostly ruled there, and were in favour with all the people, and that Earl Paul, his father, cared little about the government. It seemed to him also that the Orkneymen were longing very little for his own return home; they had then good peace, and thought, if Hakon returned, discord and strife would arise. Also it seemed to Hakon not unlikely that his own kinsmen would keep him out of the government. He took counsel, therefore, to seek help from his kinsman, King Magnus, to place him in the government of Orkney. Hakon urged King Magnus to go a-hosting to Scotland and Ireland and then to England to avenge King Harald Sigurdsson.

The King answered: "You must consider this, Hakon. If I listened to your request and went with an army across the sea, might it not take you by surprise, if I put forward a strong claim to those kingdoms beyond the sea, and did it without regarding the claim of any man?"

When Hakon heard this, he grew cold and was hardly pleased, but King Magnus ordered a levy of men and ships over all Norway.

Of the conduct of Magnus in his early manhood.
Now we shall turn to the man about whom this history was written, the holy Magnus; for you have already heard how he was well-behaved in all his conduct and unlike other young men in his growing up. But as it is the way with many to shape their conduct after their companions, and he who touches pitch is defiled by it, so when Magnus had almost reached full manhood, he was placed in the midst of fierce and wicked men,

who were ill-disposed towards good morals, in-
firm in faith, opposed to just laws, stiff-necked in
learning, tolerant of evil ways, quarrelsome and
disobedient towards the commandments of God.
So Magnus seemed, for some years, to be like
wicked men, and he lived like a viking with
robbers or soldiers, by rape and plunder, and stood
by with others at murders. We can believe that he
did this more from the wickedness and urging of
evil men than from his own badness. It seems
most likely that this viking period of Magnus' life
was at the time when his kinsmen, Hakon and
Erling, were all together in Orkney, for later no
occasion can be found for it.

*How Magnus was forced to join the host of Magnus
Barelegs; of his conduct during battle; and how he
escaped back to Scotland; and of the death of his father,
Erlend.*

At the time to which we have now come in
the story, there came west from Norway King
Magnus Barelegs with countless ships and many
troops. Many of his vassals followed: Vidkunn
Jonsson, Serk of Sogn, Kali of Agde, Saebjörn's
son, and Kol, his son, and many other chiefs. The
king intended, in this hosting, to subdue and

harry the western lands, England and Ireland, as
was said before. When King Magnus came to
Orkney, he took the Earls, Erlend and Paul, and
drove them out of the islands and sent them east
to Norway, and set Sigurd his son over Orkney,
and gave him councillors, as he was not older than
nine winters. Magnus and Erling, Erlend's sons,
and Hakon, Paul's son, he ordered to go with him
on the hosting.

Now Magnus Erlendsson was tall in stature,
bold and fleet and of great strength, of a goodly
countenance, fair of complexion, and well-
shapen in limb, noble in bearing, and most cour-
teous in all his demeanour. King Magnus made
him his table-swain, and he served continually at
the King's table.

King Magnus sailed from Orkney to the Hebrides and subdued in this expedition all the
Hebrides to his rule, and took prisoner Lawman,
Gudrod's son, the king of the Hebrides. Thence
he voyaged south to Wales and had there a great
fight in the Menai Strait with two Welsh Earls,
Hugh the Stout, and Hugh the Brave. But when
men picked up their weapons, and got them
ready for the fight, Magnus Erlendsson sat down
in the foredeck, where he would often sit, and did

not arm himself. The king inquired why he did so.

St Magnus answered: "Here I have nothing against any man, and therefore I will not fight."

"Go, then, below," said the king, "and do not lie here under men's feet, if you dare not fight, for I do not think you do this because of your religion."

Magnus, the Earl's son, remained in the same place, and took a psalter and sang during the battle, but did not shelter himself. The battle was hard and long. At last Hugh the Brave fell and the Welsh fled; and King Magnus got the victory, but had lost many good men, and many others were wounded. Magnus Erlendsson was not wounded in the fight, though he did not shelter himself. And, as could be seen by all, it was clearly miraculous that in so thick a flight of arrows and so heavy a meeting of weapons, he was not wounded, while on all sides around him armed men were falling.

King Magnus was not pleased, however, and laid on Magnus, the Earl's son, great feud and dislike on account of it. And when the holy Magnus saw that it would not be for his honour or salvation to remain longer with King Magnus,

he took further counsel with himself to do what
God taught him.

It was one night, when King Magnus lay off
Scotland, that Magnus Erlendsson stole away from
the King's ship, and so arranged his bed, that it
seemed as though a man lay there. In the morning,
when the King was dressed, he inquired if Magnus
Erlendsson was sick. He was then inquired for and
was missed. The King then had a search made for
him, but he was not found. Then the King caused
the bloodhounds to be let loose on the land.
Magnus, the Earl's son, had hurt his foot when he
leapt ashore, and the bloodhounds at once found
the scent. Magnus had made for the woods and
climbed up into a tree. The hounds came to the
oak and climbed up into it. Magnus then struck
one of them with a staff he held, and they imme-
diately took to flight with their tails between their
legs, and ran for the ships. Magnus Erlendsson
hid himself in the wood while the King's men
searched for him. He then travelled up the country and came to the court of Malcolm, King of
the Scots, and dwelt there for a while.

The same autumn King Magnus sailed back to
the Hebrides, and was there through the winter.
Early in spring he crossed to Orkney. There he

heard from Norway of the death of the Earls;
Erlend had died at Nidross and was buried there;
and Paul at Bergen. Some say that Erling, Erlend's
son, and brother to St Magnus, fell in the Menai
Strait; but Snorri Sturlasson says he fell in Ulster
with King Magnus. For when King Magnus had
ruled nine winters in Norway, he set out west to
Ireland with a great army, and during the following summer he fell in Ulster on Bartholomew's
day. And Sigurd, his son at once left Orkney for
Norway, and was there made king along with his
brothers Eystein and Olaf.

When the holy Magnus was in Scotland, he
heard of the death of Earl Erlend, his father, and
the other tidings which have been recounted
above. And when he had stayed as long in the
Scots King's court as pleased him, honoured with
the King's gifts and a noble retinue, he travelled
to Caithness, and there was well received, honoured and esteemed by all, and at once chosen
and ennobled with the title of "Earl," beloved and
honoured of all the friends of God.

Thereafter, without delay, the holy Earl Magnus was made Paul out of Saul, a preacher from a
man-slayer, and he avenged on himself the early
wrongdoing of his life.

How Hakon returned and captured all of Orkney; and how Magnus claimed his patrimony which was granted to him by the Norwegian kings; and the two earls ruled peacefully in Orkney together.

A winter or two after King Magnus Barelegs fell, Hakon Paulsson went east over the sea to Norway, and the kings gave him the title of Earl, and such possessions as came to him by birth. He then returned west over the sea and took to himself all the government of Orkney, and with such great and aggressive greed that he slew without cause the steward of the King of Norway, who held and governed that part of the islands which the holy Magnus inherited, and in that way took possession of all the Orkney islands by sheer force; for half of the islands belonged to Magnus as his patrimony. Now when the holy Magnus heard with what violence and injustice Hakon, his cousin, had seized his hereditary lands, he took counsel with his men as to what he should do. It was agreed among them that he should wait a while, in order for the anger and greed of Hakon, his kinsman, to abate, and so that it might not appear that he sought his inheritance by arms, but as a friend and dear lover of law and justice.

Now when the time was come that the holy

Magnus wished to visit his patrimony, he journeyed with a noble company from Caithness to
Orkney, and his kinsmen and friends were glad of
his return. He asked to take possession of his
patrimony. This was well pleasing to the franklins;
for he was well loved; and he had many kinsmen
and connections who were anxious to help him
to hold his dominions. Thora, his mother, was
then married to a man named Sigurd; they owned
a large farm in Paplay.

When Earl Hakon heard that Magnus had
come into the islands, he gathered an army around him, and wished not to give up the government, but to defend it. The friends of both then
journeyed between them, and tried to make
peace. So it came to pass, through good counsel,
that they were reconciled on the condition that
Earl Hakon should give up half the kingdom if it
were so decided by the King of Norway.

Magnus Erlendsson sailed at once east to Norway to seek King Eystein; for King Sigurd was
then absent on a journey to Jerusalem. King
Eystein received the young lord Magnus exceed-
ingly well, and gave up to him his patrimony, the
half of Orkney, and therewith he received the title
of Earl in Orkney from the Kings, along with very

handsome presents. And after this the lord Earl
Magnus returned west over the sea to his dominions, and his friends and kinsmen were glad and
with them all the people. Then there was much
good fellowship between him and Earl Hakon for
many winters, which their friends brought about.
There was then plenty and peace in Orkney
while their friendship held.

The kinsmen, lord Earl Magnus and Hakon,
provided for the land defence together for a while,
so closely were they agreed.

*Of the rule and conduct of the Lord Magnus; and of
his marriage.*

Lord Magnus was a man the most renowned in
his rule and authority, dignified and upright, a
steadfast friend and brave, skilled in feats of arms
and blessed with victory in battle, gentle in peace,
yet a strong ruler, condescending in speech, and
clement, prudent in counsel, and had every man's
praise. He was open-handed with his money, and
generous among chieftains. Every day he gave
great help to poor men for the love of God. He
punished much harrying and theft, and caused
vikings and ill-doers, rich as well as poor, to be
slain. No respecter of persons was he in his

judgments; he respected God's law more than differences of estate among them. In all things he observed strictly the commandments of God, and was unsparing towards himself. Many were the excellent virtues which he manifested before God, but hid from men.

But since the holy Earl Magnus had rule and government over worldly folk, he desired to be like the great ones of the earth in the customs of life; he took and betrothed himself to a high-born princess, and the fairest maiden of the most noble house of the chiefs of Scotland, and brought her home with him and married her. He dwelt ten years with this virgin, pure and unstained of all the pollution of sin. And when he felt within himself the temptation to fleshly lust, he plunged into cold water and sought help from God.

Now the enemy of all mankind stirred up temptations and hot persecutions on every side against this knight of God, sowing discord and hatred among brethren and kinsmen and dear friends, all to hinder him, and to bring to naught his good deeds, which then began to increase with him. It must next be set down how this discord was made between the Earls.

*Of the discord that arose between the two earls; and
how the Lord Magnus went away to the English court
to escape from malice and wickedness.*

When the kinsmen, Earl Magnus and Earl Hakon,
had for some winters ruled their lands in peace
and good agreement, it came to pass, as it often
does, that evil disposed men began to destroy their
brotherly concord. Earl Hakon then drew towards those evil men, for the kinsmen were very
unlike in temper. Lord Earl Magnus was benevo-
lent and faithful in his promises; he wished to
retain the kingdom which God had given to him,
and desired nothing more. For in what way could
he be proved to desire other men's kingdoms or
possessions, who was so free with his own flesh,
that he did not spare his life for the love of God?
He reformed his subjects and accustomed them
to right living, so that after he had delivered and
given peace to his kingdom from the aggressions
of wicked vikings, he did not allow any of his men
to go a-hosting, and punished severely all lawless-
ness and wickedness.

But Earl Hakon was hard-hearted and cruel,
greedy both of wealth and power, and more
prone to urge his men to go a-hosting than to
prevent them, and punished little wickedness and

ill-doing. He was jealous of his cousin's liberality
and popular favour and would willingly over-
come and subdue his kingdom with pillage and
injustice, and began to plot against his life with
treacherous cunning.

Now when the blessed Magnus had become
aware that Hakon was plotting to deprive him of
his life and kingdom, he took counsel with his
advisors, and it seemed to them that he ought to
give way for a little to Hakon's malice and fury.
He then chose the best of his followers to accompany him, and sailed to England and sought a
meeting with King Henry, son of William the
Bastard, who was then sole king over England.

When the holy Magnus was come to this King,
he made known to him the occasion and object
of his coming. And the King received him with
great honour; and into so great a friendship did
he rise with the King, that he maintained him and
all his people at his own cost for twelve months
magnificently, as it was fitting for a King to treat
a famous leader. But this holy man held himself
and his retinue so wisely, that he shunned all
fellowship with wicked men.

And when the lord King learned from his
prudence, how Earl Magnus was a doer of good

works and of seemly manners, and that the Holy
Spirit dwelt in him, he earnestly gave heed to his
counsel, and followed his advice. And that he
might not for the future stain his chastity by
consenting to other men's sins, Magnus made
ready his home-going as soon as the twelve
months were passed, which he had spent with
King Henry.

*How Magnus returned home to claim his own; and
made a new reconciliation with Hakon to divide the
earldom.*

After Magnus had taken leave of King Henry,
honoured with many rich gifts, and esteemed and
glorified by the Lord King, they parted with the
greatest love and friendship. He visited first all the
holy places which were near, and then travelled
home to his own land. But while the holy Magnus
was abroad, Earl Hakon with great greed and
harrying had subdued not only all the Orkney
islands, but all Caithness as well, with robbery and
violence; and so it came to pass, that Hakon sat at
that time in Caithness, when the holy Earl Magnus landed in Orkney with five ships well manned
with valiant and well armed men, meaning to get
back his kingdom. He did this, though, with no

false passion of this world's ambition, nor greed
of unlawful possession, especially when he had
already so long desired God, and was wholly
taken up out of the longing for mortal things into
the desire for eternal joy.

The tidings of his return home were at once
told on all sides. Earl Hakon summoned to him
cruel ill-doers who always and everywhere have
wrought evil from their very birth. Hakon meant
then to come unawares upon the holy Magnus,
and so accomplish the treachery which he had
long had in mind. But the Supreme Heavenly
King, who from eternity had ordained that He
would keep His glorious chosen vessel in His
treasuries, saw in this man of His own election
some imperfection still of worldly behaviour
which needed to be purified. Thus it came to pass
that the Earls sent their most prudent counsellors
between themselves with messages for peace and
reconciliation.

It came about then, through the intervention
of good men, that a reconciliation was made
between the kinsmen in this way, that the earldom
of Orkney, Caithness, and Shetland should be
divided between the Earls Magnus and Hakon,
and that neither should assail the other's kingdom.

When this agreement had been made and confirmed with oaths, the Earls met with the kiss of
peace. But all that the holy Earl Magnus intended
for peace, Hakon turned to deceit and cunning.
And the longer he retained the poison of evil, the
more wickedly did he spew it up, for his wickedness and villainy increased so much as time went
on, that he could no longer hide it.

The holy Earl Magnus then began again to rule
his kingdom with peace and joy for a time. And
it is known best in the sight of God how holily
he lived in this biding of his death; how he
adorned himself with the exercise of every kind
of grace, in prayer and searchings of heart, in
purity and nobleness, in alms-giving, and in all
gentleness towards his people, in afflictions and
manifold sufferings, which he endured in his
body, and in many other virtues. As every holy
man of God does, in the same way Earl Magnus
prepared for his martyrdom; the story of which
we shall now with God's help begin.

*How the two Earls came together to battle at Hrossey;
and how a conditional peace was made between them.*
When the above-mentioned reconciliation and
peace had lasted between the Earls some winters,

Hakon showed himself treacherous by pouring out from his breast the great wickedness, which he had for a time held back.

Two men were with Earl Hakon who are mentioned as by far the worst in coming between the kinsmen: the one was called Sigurd; the other Sigvat Sokki. Sigurd had a brother, called Thorstein, who was the most faithful follower of Earl Magnus. Many others there were who had an evil hand in this matter, and these were all with Hakon, for Magnus would keep no slanderer among his followers. These slanderings went so far that the Earls gathered their troops together, and each fared against the other with a great following. They both made their way to the island of Hrossey, for there was the Thingstead* of the Orkney islands. And when they had come there, each of them drew up his army in battle array.

There had come all the men of rank with the Earls, and many were friends of both. And because many well disposed men were anxious to prevent strife between them, they bound themselves to keep the peace by oaths and handsellings at the witness of the best men. It was settled they should

* Place for the parliament gathering.

meet in the spring in Egilsay after Easter. At this
meeting each Earl was to have two ships and an
equal number of men. Both Earls took oaths to
have and hold the agreement which the best men
should settle at that meeting to declare between
them. And after this was done each left for his
own home.

Of Hakon's treacherous plotting against the holy Mag-
nus; and of their coming to Egilsay, and the omen of
the wave.

With this conditional reconciliation the holy
Magnus was well pleased, as he was thoroughly
wholehearted and of good conscience. But Earl
Hakon had at this meeting glossed over his
treachery and hid it with a cloud of hypocrisy;
for this agreement he had made with deceit and
treachery, as was afterwards proved; for at the time
Hakon and his wicked servants conspired together for the slaughter and death of the holy
Magnus. Therefore they settled among themselves that this crime should no longer be delayed,
and that now they would fully slake their cruel
thirst with the shedding of blood.

As soon as Easter time was passed, each of the
two made ready for this meeting in different ways.

The holy Magnus called to him all the men whom he knew had the most goodwill to make things better between the kinsmen. He had two longships manned with the bravest men, as many as were agreed upon. And when he was ready he held to the island of Egilsay. But as they were rowing on a calm sea and in still weather, there rose a wave beside the ship in which Earl Magnus was, and broke over the place where the Earl was sitting. The chief men in Earl Magnus's ship were called: Thorstein, who was mentioned before, Arnkell, Grim, and Gilli, and many other doughty men. They marvelled greatly that the wave fell on them in a calm sea, where no wave had fallen before, and where the water was deep.

Then the holy Earl Magnus said: "It is not strange though you wonder at this. But my thought is, that this is a foreboding of the end of my life. Maybe that will happen here, which was augured, that Earl Paul's son will perpetrate the greatest crime and is plotting treachery against us at this meeting."

Earl Magnus's men were much distressed when he spoke of so speedy expectation of his death, and prayed him to take care of himself and guard his life, and have no faith in Earl Hakon.

Earl Magnus replied: "I shall certainly go to this meeting, as was agreed upon, and make no breach of my promise for the sake of a mere foreboding. And let all be as God wills about our voyage. But if there be any choice, then would I much rather suffer wrong than do it to another. So may God let Hakon get forgiveness, though he do me wrong."

Of the host that came to Egilsay with Hakon, in violation of the oath; and of the discourse between Magnus and Hakon.

Now it is to be told of Earl Hakon, that he called to him a great army. He had seven or eight warships, all of great size, manned with troops; all the men were well armed as if they were going to battle. But when the force came together, then Earl Hakon made it clear before his men, that at this meeting it should be so settled with Magnus, that they should not both rule from that time forth. Many of the Earl's men, who might truly be called children of the devil, expressed delight at this purpose; but Sigurd and Sigvat Sokki were still giving the worst advice and ever urging on to wickedness. The men then began to row fast, and went furiously and with great speed.

Havard Gunnisson, who was spoken of before, was with Earl Hakon; he was a close friend of both Earls. Hakon had hid from him this bad counsel. But as soon as he was aware of it, he leapt overboard from the Earl's ship and swam to an island; for he would be in no treachery against the holy Magnus. That man was with Earl Magnus, who was called Holdbodi, a trustworthy franklin from the Hebrides; he was Earl Magnus's most dear follower. He was near by all that happened, and has since most clearly related the dealings and all the discourse of Earls Hakon and Magnus, which may here be heard next.

The holy Earl Magnus came sooner to Egilsay with his men than Hakon. And when they saw Hakon's eight warships, Earl Magnus thought he knew that treachery was being prepared, and all the men, who had any insight saw well that such a multitude of armed men was not wanted for a peaceful purpose. When the holy Earl Magnus saw that the treachery of Hakon was about to show itself, he went with his men up into the island to a church to pray, and was there through the night, not because of fear or dread, but rather to commit all his care to God. His men offered to defend him, and fight against Hakon.

But he answered: "I will not place your lives in danger for me. And if peace cannot be made between us two kinsmen, then let it be as God wills; for rather will I suffer evil and treachery than do it to others."

For this noble martyr knew that all guile and deceit is returned to him who does it. Now his men saw the truth of what he had said to them before about the treachery of Hakon. But as Earl Magnus knew before of his death, whether through foresight or divine revelation, he wished neither to fly nor to go far from the meeting of his enemies, and he went to the holy church for no other reason than for religion. Earl Magnus watched long in prayer during the night and meditated on his salvation, and prayed earnestly; he committed all his cause and himself into the hands of God. In the morning he let Mass be sung, and received in that Mass the *Corpus Domini*.

The same morning that Earl Hakon had come up on to the island with his ill-doers, he sent four of his men who were the fiercest and most eager to work ill, to seize Earl Magnus wherever he was. These four, who, from their ferocity and thirsting for bloodshed, may rather be called the wildest wolves than rational men, leapt into the church just as Mass was ending. They at once snatched the holy Earl Magnus with great violence and clamour, out of the peace and bosom of Holy Church.

The saint was held in the thralls of sin, the righteous was bound, dragged unjustly by the unjust, and then led away before the greedy judge, Earl Hakon. But this strong champion had such great steadfastness that neither his body shook from fear, nor his mind from dread or grief, for he forsook this thorny world with all its fruitless flowers. He hoped that God would recompense his patience with an ineffable crown; but their cruelty and fury with everlasting torture in the fire of hell, because of their inhuman wickedness and monstrous greed. He was as glad and cheerful when they took him, as if he had been bidden to a banquet, and had so settled a heart and mind that he spoke to his enemies with no bitterness, anger, or tremor in his voice.

When the holy Earl Magnus was brought before Earl Hakon, he said to Hakon with great calmness: "You do not well, kinsman, when you keep not your oath, and it is much to be looked for that you did this more from the malice and urging on of others than from your own ill-will.

Now I will make to you three offers, that you may take one of them rather than break your oath."

Earl Hakon said: "I will first hear what you offer."

Magnus said: "This is the first offer, that I shall travel abroad to Rome or as far as Jerusalem, to seek the holy places, and so make atonement for both of us; I will take two ships out of the land furnished with good men and the necessary equipment. I will swear never to come to Orkney again."

This offer was quickly refused by Hakon and his men.

Then Earl Magnus said: "Now since our life is in your power, and I know that in many things I have offended against Almighty God, and have need to make amends, send me to Scotland to the friends of us both, and let me be there in ward with two men with me for company; and see you so to it that I may never come forth of that wardship without your leave."

This they at once rejected and found many reasons why it could not be.

Then the brave Earl spoke again: "Now is my choice very limited," he said. "Now is there but one choice left, which I will offer you, and God knows that I am more concerned for your salvation here, than for the life of my body; for, after all, it beseems you little to take my life. Let me be maimed in my limbs, or let my eyes be put out, and set me so in a dark dungeon, whence I may never come out."

Then said Earl Hakon: "This offer I take, and no more do I ask." ·

Then leapt up Earl Hakon's men and said: "In this finding we do not agree, to torture Earl Magnus: but one or the other of you two we will slay; and from this day you shall not both of you reign over these lands."

Then said Earl Hakon: "Rather will I rule the lands than die at once, if you are so strict in this matter."

So tells Holdbodi of their parley.

After this Magnus fell to prayers and bowed his face into his hands and shed many tears before God, giving his cause, his life, and himself, into the power of the Lord.

Of the death of the holy Magnus.
After this, when the holy friend of God, Earl Magnus, was condemned and doomed to death, Earl Hakon bade Ofeig, his standard-bearer, slay

Earl Magnus; but he refused with greatest anger.
Then Earl Hakon compelled his cook, who was
called Lifolf, to smite Earl Magnus, but he began
to weep aloud.

Then Earl Magnus said to him: "Weep not; for
there is fame to you in doing this. Be of steadfast
mind, for you shall have my clothes as is the
custom and law of the men of old. You shall not
be afraid, for you do this by force, and he that
forces you to it has more sin than you."

And when he had said this, he took off his kirtle
and gave it to Lifolf. Then the blessed Earl Magnus
begged leave to pray first, and it was granted him.
He fell to the ground and gave himself into the
power of God, offering himself to Him in sacri-
fice. He prayed not only for himself, but rather
for his enemies and murderers as well; and he
forgave them all with his whole heart that which
they were wrongdoing against him; and he con-
fessed all his sins to God, and prayed that they
might all be washed away by the shedding of his
blood; and he commended his spirit into the
hands of God, praying God's angels to come to
meet it, and bear it to the rest of Paradise.

Then when this noble martyr of God had
ended his prayer, he said to Lifolf: "Stand before

me and hew me on the head a great wound; for it is not right to behead chiefs like thieves. Be strong, man, and weep not, for I have prayed God to pardon you."

After this Earl Magnus crossed himself, and bowed himself to the stroke. Lifolf struck him on the head a great blow with an axe.

Then Earl Hakon said: "Strike again."

Then Lifolf struck into the same wound. Then the holy Earl Magnus fell on his knees, and with this martyrdom passed from the miseries of this world to the everlasting joys of the kingdom of heaven. And him whom the murderer dispatched from this earth, Almighty God let reign with Him in heaven. His body fell to the earth, but his spirit was gloriously taken up into the heavenly glory of the angels. The spot where the holy Earl Magnus was slain was stony and mossy. But soon his merits before God were made manifest, as since then there is in that place a green field, fair and smooth, and God showed by this token, that Earl Magnus was slain for righteousness' sake, and gained the fairness and greenness of Paradise in the land of the living.

The day of the holy Magnus' death is two nights after the feast of Tiburtius and Valerianus;

it was on the second day of the week that the
worthy Earl Magnus was slain, the third week
after Lady Day in Lent. He had then been twelve
winters Earl with Hakon. Then Sigurd the Cru-
sader, and his brothers Eystein and Olaf were
Kings in Norway. There had passed since the
death of the holy Olaf Haraldsson, seventy-four
years [eighty-six]. It was in the days of Pope
Paschal, the second of that name, and of St Jon
Bishop of Holar in Iceland.

In honour of the holy Earl Magnus thus speaks
Master Robert who edited this history in Latin:

"To-day shines upon us, dearest brethren, the
day of the death of the blessed Earl Magnus the
Martyr, the day of his rest and of his eternal joy.
This glorious martyr of God, the blessed Earl
Magnus, adorned with the crown of his own
blood, suffered after the incarnation of our Lord
Jesus Christ, one thousand one hundred and four
[sixteen] years, on Monday the sixteenth of the
calends of May. Let us follow the way of his life;
let us hold to the example of his works. Let us
strive to make our lives like his. This grant us the
Lord Jesus Christ, who is the honour and blessing,
the help and salvation, the gladness and glory of
all His holy and righteous men; who with the

Father and Holy Ghost lives and reigns, One God in Three Persons, world without end. Amen."

Master Robert wrote this history in Latin to the worship and honour of the holy Magnus, Earl of the Isles, twenty years after the date of his martyrdom.

How the Lord Magnus' mother sought the body of her son to have Christian burial; and of his grave at Birsay; and how Earl Hakon ruled thenceforth.

Now we must take up the story again, and tell of the things which were done after the death of the holy Earl Magnus. So great was the fierceness and cruelty of Earl Hakon, and so great his anger and fury at the blessed Magnus, that he bore not less malice to Earl Magnus dead than living. And though the anger and fury of most men can be abated after the doing of their ill deed, the ill will and malice in the heart of Hakon took no rest; for he forbade Earl Magnus to be buried at the Church as Christian men, but ordered that he should be hidden there in the ground where he was slain.

It had been agreed at the first meeting of the Earls in Hrossey, that when their reconciliation had been fully made and confirmed as the best

men determined, as they had bound themselves
by oaths, that both Earls, when they fared from
the meeting, which was fixed to be held in Egilsay,
should go to a feast in Paplay at Thora's, the
mother of Earl Magnus. But now, after the slaying
and death of the Earl, Earl Hakon went to the
banquet with his men. The feast was of the best.

Now when drink took hold on Earl Hakon,
then Thora went to him and said: "You have come
here alone, lord; but I expected both of you, you
and Earl Magnus my son. Now listen to my prayer
as you will that Almighty God shall hear yours at
doomsday; grant to me that my son may be buried
at church."

Earl Hakon looked on her, and shed tears,
and said: "Bury your son, woman, where you
will."

Earl Magnus was then borne to the church, and
buried in Birsay, at Christ's Kirk, which Earl
Thorfinn, his grandfather, let be built. Immedi-
ately a heavenly light was often seen to shine over
his grave. Then men began to call upon the holy
Earl Magnus, when they were placed in danger,
and he met their need as they prayed. Always was
a heavenly odour perceived at his grave, and there
sick men obtained health. Next, sick men made

journeys from Orkney and Shetland, who were hopeless of cure, and watched before his tomb, and were cured of all their diseases, but still men did not dare to make known the miracles of Earl Magnus while Earl Hakon lived. So it is told, that the men who had been worst between the Earls and most in treachery towards Earl Magnus, came most of them to speedy ends and short life, and died a shameful death.

After the death of Magnus, Hakon Paulsson took possession of all the Earldom of the Orkney islands. He compelled all men to swear oath and fealty to himself, as well those who before had served Earl Magnus. He became great, and laid heavy burdens on the friends of Earl Magnus, whom he thought had been most against himself in their negotiations.

Some winters after, Hakon made ready to go abroad. He went south to Rome, and on that journey went all the way to Jerusalem, as was then the custom for palmers. He sought the holy places, and bathed in the river Jordan. After that he returned to his own land and took up the government in Orkney. He then became a good ruler, and established good peace in his kingdom. He made new laws, which the franklins liked

much better than those which had been before.
By such things he began to increase his popularity.
So it came to pass that the people of Orkney
would have no other than Earl Hakon and his
offspring to hold rule among them. And here is
the end of what is to be said about Hakon in this
book.

*Of the miracles at the grave of the holy Magnus; and
how Bishop William was brought to acknowledge his
holiness, and enshrined his relics.*

At this time William was bishop in Orkney.★ The
bishop's seat was then at Christ's Kirk in Birsay
where the holy Earl Magnus was buried; he
doubted long about his holiness and kept down
this new thing, that is, the miraculous virtue
experienced at the grave of Magnus.

Bergfinn Starrisson was the name of a franklin
north in Shetland. He was sightless, and fared
south to Orkney and watched at the tomb of the
Earl Magnus. With him watched two men, one
was named Sigurd and the other Thorbjorn; they
were both cripples. Earl Magnus appeared to
them and made them quite cured. Again twenty-

★ The following paragraphs are taken from the Lesser Saga in order to fill
the gap which occurs here in the Greater Saga.

four men watched at the tomb of Earl Magnus
and all got healing for their hurts.

Many men recounted this before Bishop William and urged him to speak about it with Paul,
Hakon's son, who then ruled over the Isles after
his father, and ask him to give leave for the sacred
relics of Earl Magnus to be taken up out of the
ground, but the bishop took that hard. Often,
though, he was reminded in dreams that he
should make up his mind about the Earl's holiness,
and yet he would not believe in it.

One summer Bishop William sailed east to
Norway on some pressing business, and immedi-
ately turned homewards in the autumn, and came
in the beginning of winter to Shetland. There he
was laid up by adverse winds and storms. But
when much of the winter passed and there was
still no fair wind for the isles, the Bishop despaired
of being able to reach his see before spring. The
captain asked him, if he were to sing Mass the
next Lord's Day at home, would he admit to the
holiness of Earl Magnus? The bishop, so to say,
gave his consent to this, but more from necessity
than of free promise. But the moment this was
done, there was calm weather and soon a fair
wind. And afterwards they sailed for Orkney,

arriving home before the next Lord's Day; and all
praised God and also his holy martyr Earl Magnus. Some men say that Bishop William still did
not agree to take out of the ground the sacred
relics of Earl Magnus until one day there at home
he could not get out of the church, for he had
become blind. He could not find the door till he
repented of his unbelief, and wept bitterly, and
besought God that he might light upon the tomb
of Earl Magnus. And when he came there, he fell
full length on the ground, and promised to at
once take out of the earth his sacred relics, when
he received his sight. And when he had ended his
prayer, he received his sight there at the tomb.

Afterwards he summoned the wisest and the
best men in Orkney, and there came a great
multitude to Christ's Kirk at Birsay. Then the
sacred relics of Earl Magnus were taken out of the
ground. The bones had risen almost to the surface
of the ground. He then had the bones washed,
and the joint of the finger taken and tested three
times in the consecrated fire. But it did not burn,
rather it became like burned silver. Some men
said it ran into the form of a cross. Then there
were many miracles done by the holy relics. After
that learned men took the holy relics and laid

I
must
tell
you
this

I know something so wonderful that I must tell you! It is so vital that it may change your entire future as it did mine. In fact, the decision you make about it will affect you both in life and death.

Let me emphasize that this message is absolutely true, because God said it. When God makes a promise you can rest upon it, because His promises can never fail. God will not make you believe this message. That is your choice, but He will hold you responsible for having heard it. It is a very personal message, something you must decide. You must say either, "I will" or "I will not."

Here is the message. It is an exact quotation from God's word, the Holy Bible. *"For God so loved the world, that he gave his only begotten Son, that whosoever believeth in him should not perish, but have everlasting life."* (John 3:16) Did you ever hear such wonderful words? Think for a moment what they say. They reveal three marvelous facts.

First, *"God so loved the world"!* Since you are in the world, He loved you. If that doesn't astonish you, remember, that when God loved you, He loved a sinner! (Romans 3:23) If you are honest, you will agree.

Although God loves you, He still hates your sin. Since God is holy, He must punish sin. He had to make a holy way of saving sinners. Otherwise, the sinner must pay for his sins, and that would mean spending eternity in hell. (Revelation 20:15)

T he second great fact is *"He gave his only begotten Son"!* God loved you so much, that He sent His Son to earth to become a man and die on the cross of Calvary, so that you could be saved.

You see, someone must pay the penalty of sin--either you or a sinless substitute. God gave His Son, Jesus Christ, to be your sinless substitute. He shed His blood so that your sins can be put away, so that you can have eternal life.

A nd now the third tremendous fact is *"Whosoever believeth in Him should not perish, but have everlasting life:!"* Think of it! God gives eternal life to those who believe in Jesus Christ. The Saviour has "finished" the work. He has died. He has risen from the grave, and He has gone back into heaven. Now your part is to believe in Him.

This simply means that you must agree that you are a sinner, realize that Christ has paid the "full" penalty for your sins, and then receive Him as your Lord and Saviour.

This is the message which I had to tell you. Now, you must make a decision. Will you accept Him, or reject Him? Think of it once again: *"For God so loved the world, that he gave his only begotten Son, that whosoever believeth in him should not perish, but have everlasting life."* (John 3:16)

Your time on earth is short, but your decision for Christ lasts for eternity. Will you receive Jesus Christ as your Saviour and be confident of everlasting life?

If you have decided to trust Jesus Christ as your Saviour after reading this tract, please write and let us know.

Name _____

Address _____

City _____ Zip _____

State _____ Age _____

FELLOWSHIP TRACT LEAGUE
P.O. BOX 164 • LEBANON, OH 45036
www.fellowshiptractleague.org © Tract 116
All tracts free as the Lord provides. Not to be sold.